Safe to Feel

Copyright @ 2019 by Phylicia Masonheimer

Available online at:
phyliciamasonheimer.com

Printed in the United States of America

*To my husband Josh, who loved me
at my worst and helps me to be my best*

SAFE TO *Feel*

A 30-DAY DEVOTIONAL FOR WOMEN
WHO STRUGGLE WITH AFFECTION

Phylicia Masonheimer

CONTENTS

Introduction   10

Averse to Affection 16
The Connection Between Anger and Fear 19
Perfect Love Casts Out Fear 22
You Are Not Enough On Your Own 25
Afraid of Falling....................................... 28
Brokenness on Display 31
Nurturing Little Loves 34
Pressing Through Shame 37
I Need to Feel Safe.................................... 40
What if I'm Rejected 43
I'm Failing at Marriage 46
Action Precedes Emotion 49
Affection is not Weakness 52
Personality is Not an Excuse 55
Acknowledging Your Own Emotions 58
Affection After Wounding 61

Accepting Grace for Your Weakness 64
Speaking a Love Language You Don't Know 67
Failure is Not the End 70
The Sex-Love Connection 73
Breaking the Hold of Insecurity 76
Showing Affection in the Community of Faith 80
Grace for Us, Grace for Others 83
When you Don't Want God as a Father 86
Intimacy When Your Spouse Isn't Helping 89
Preach Truth to Yourself 92
Think About Such Things 95
Affirm Your Progress 98
Change the Narrative 101
Your are a Fearless Women of God 104
Twenty Ways to Grow in Affection Today 108

Introduction

I am not good at hugging.

My friends know this and it has become something of a joke among us: "Phy hugs like a praying mantis" is a common tease when we get together. For most of my life I just accepted I was bad at affection. I didn't ask questions; I didn't dig into *why* I disliked hugs or being touched.

Marriage forced me to acknowledge this area that for so long went unaddressed. My husband and I are opposites on every personality test, including the Five Love Languages. If you're not familiar, the love languages are five ways you express or receive love from your spouse (or anyone, for that matter). I love to receive gifts and spend quality time. Josh loves quality time and physical affection.

A few years into our marriage, with the honeymoon stage officially over, I reverted back to my comfortable patterns of behavior – patterns which excluded affection. After our first daughter was born, we went *weeks* without kissing or touching one another. I wasn't being malicious. *I just didn't think of it.* These things didn't even register as a need to me. Josh, however, was withering up inside, feeling unloved and unwanted. He wanted affection. I didn't know how to give it. When we talked about it, I became inflammatory and angry. I felt like he was asking me to give something I was incapable of providing.

It's important to note that physical affection as a love language – and as discussed in this devotional – does not refer to sex. When I mention intimacy, I'm referring to emotional and spiritual intimacy, not sexual. I also want to make an important point: I am assuming that those attempting to implement what I share here are in *generally healthy Christian marriages.* If you are experiencing abuse, please contact a trusted person in your life.

Back to intimacy: In my own marriage, sex was never the problem. Josh and I have had a healthy sex life for most of our marriage. Our problem – *my* problem – was *intimacy.* If you've only understood intimacy as a pseudonym for sex, it's so much more than that. Webster's defines it as "close familiarity, attachment, togetherness, confidentiality." It's a deep, close relationship with another person.

In my first book, *Christian Cosmo: The Sex Talk You Never Had*, I opened up about my history of sexual addiction from age twelve into my early twenties. For most of my life I saw my sexual issues as something sequestered into a corner of my existence, but as most of us know, sin never stays in a corner. I learned about sex through an erotic romance novel and expanded my knowledge in the throes of addiction. This meant sex, to me, was always about passion and "heat," never about love and affection. I didn't realize the damage that was done while I was a child. Only when I became a married woman, attempting to understand a physical relationship apart from the sexual act, did I see the impact of sexual sin on marriage.

I wish I could say I started asking questions in that first hard season, but I didn't. I decided Josh was needy, and the very idea of being affectionate made me so uncomfortable I just avoided the issue altogether. Naturally, this did not improve our marriage. Fast forward to after our second daughter was born: I desperately wanted our marriage to improve. Josh was making efforts, but every time I tried to reciprocate, my whole being felt held back. I felt like there was a wall between my emotions and my true self. One morning as I prayed about it, the Lord revealed the root of my aversion to affection: *Fear.*

Most people would never consider me a fearful person; people describe me as confident, bold, and fear*less*. But in this area of my life, I was crippled by fear. Fear of rejection. Fear of intimacy. Fear of trying and failing. I was so completely afraid of giving affection that I didn't even try. But even more than my fear, I had a deep desire to feel *safe*. If I didn't feel safe, I was unlikely to express emotion and physical affection. So when my husband and I were at odds, I did not feel safe from *rejection* – so I didn't show physical *affection*.

There was also a measure of fear over being "weak": If I allowed myself to feel, and to express my feelings physically, would I still be a strong woman? The walls around my heart were so high after years of protecting myself from rejection.

I needed to be *safe to feel*.

This epiphany began my search through the Word and online for resources about affection and fear of intimacy. There are some fascinating psychological reports I recommend Googling. In this devotional, however, I'm taking a spiritual approach. The psychological reasons behind our fear of physical touch are helpful, but that is not what helped me grow in this area. My walk with God is what freed me from fear.

I wrote this little book as a heart-to-heart from one struggling woman to another. Much of it will simply share what I have learned in this journey. I'm not going to give you many action items, because heart change has to happen before action can take place! Rather, here is what I hope you do these next thirty days:

• **Read the short chapter and ask, "Does any of this resonate with me? Have these thoughts or feelings entered my mind?"**
• **Read the daily verse and pray, "God, how does this truth address my deepest fears?"**
• **Challenge yourself:** *What would happen if I stepped out in courage and let God free me from my fear of intimacy?*

It took months for me to really make progress in this area of my life, so I don't expect you to find freedom in thirty days! My goal is to push you to our Savior, who truly overcomes the world – including the fears of our hurting hearts.

CHAPTER ONE

AVERSE TO AFFECTION

Do you pull back when someone initiates a hug? Forget to kiss your husband? Feel weird about embracing your kids? When you meet people do you say, "I'm not a hugger?"

When I first opened up about my own struggle with affection, dozens of women responded with, "**me too!**" I had no idea so many women battled with this aversion. Most of us simply accept that this is who we are, not bothering to ask questions or probe deeper into our own hearts.

This month, I'm asking *you* to ask those questions. Together we're going to probe deeper into your heart, uncovering the reasons you withhold affection from those closest to you. Perhaps, like me, you watch other people with sadness or jealousy, wishing you could give yourself as freely. Perhaps – like me! – you feel an emotional wall rise up the second you try. People who don't struggle with affection don't really understand this, and probably advise you to "just do it" (there is a little truth to this, as we will talk about later, but motives must be addressed first). Before we step out and challenge ourselves, though, we need to do some heart work. Or rather, we need to invite the Holy Spirit to do it for us.

As believers in Jesus we are given a Helper, God's Spirit, who declares truth to us and enables us to live out an overcoming Christian life (John 16:33). Chances are you've already tried overcoming this on your own wisdom and effort – it doesn't work long term. You burn out, or feel overwhelmed, or end up right where you were before. It is God's Spirit who does the work in our hearts, minds, and emotions, enabling us to overcome our reservations and give affection even when we feel unequipped.

The Spirit began this work in me long ago, but it took years of growing with Him, learning to listen to His voice, and diligently spending time in the Word before I realized the role affection would play in my life and family. Day by day He showed me that my aversion to affection wasn't just my personality; it was something God desired to refine and sanctify. He wanted to free me from bondage. And He has!

The question I want you to ask today is: *When did I first notice I didn't like affection?* Were you a child? A teen? Was it toward everyone, or just a specific person? Did it start because of a childhood wound, a poor parental relationship, or an incident of abuse?

Then today, meditate on John 16:33. To meditate is to "think about"; to absorb into your mind, to remember and rehearse to yourself. Scripture calls us to meditate on God's Word (Joshua 1:8, Psalm 1:2). Today, remember that you are not alone in this struggle. The Spirit is already working in you for healing.

> *"When the Spirit of truth comes, he will guide you into all the truth, for he will not speak on his own authority, but whatever he hears he will speak, and he will declare to you the things that are to come."*
>
> –John 16:33

CHAPTER TWO

THE CONNECTION BETWEEN ANGER & FEAR

I have a temper. Anger comes easily to me, just as depression or anxiety come easily to others. I particularly hate being interrupted when I'm working, and in a season of small children, that's pretty much all day except nap time! God has used my season to teach me a lot about grace: The grace He shows me, and the grace I need to show others.

My anger was another "personality trait" I wrote off when first married. My husband is one of the calmest, most patient men I know, but even he was pushed away by my zero-to-sixty emotions. During one particular fight – the kind where you go in circles, never really getting anywhere – I shouted, "I just need to know I'm

enough!" We both stopped. I'd never expressed that to him - or to anyone, for that matter. I didn't even know I was *afraid* of being "not enough." This moment was pivotal, because while we continued to struggle with anger in our marriage for a few more years, I saw the connection between my anger and my fear.

When we are afraid we respond reactively, not rationally. Until we can look at a situation objectively our emotions will do the "thinking" for us. Anger is often a gut-level response to fear of loss, fear of intimacy, or fear of failure. In my case, I lashed out when Josh wasn't happy because I thought it was a reflection of my own failure as a wife. Anger is not a welcoming emotion and my husband naturally pulled away from me. This made me feel **more** like a failure, which made me **more** angry – at myself, but manifested at him. What a crazy cycle!

What does anger have to do with affection? I think the two are more connected than we think. When we feel like we're failing at affection, we get angry: First at ourselves, then at others for exposing our failure. Then our anger pushes our loved ones *further* away, which leads us to despair. We decide to make a little effort to hug or kiss in hopes of restoring connection. But when our loved one doesn't respond the way we hope, we get embarrassed, feel like we've failed, get mad – and the cycle starts all over again.

Have you experienced this cycle? Yours might look a little different. Think for a moment about your temper. Do you struggle with anger? If so, ask yourself: *What am I afraid of losing when I get angry?*

Is it approval? Is it love? Is it control? Do you think, if your spouse ignores your attempt to hug them, that you're losing their love? If you do, you may react in fear. The emotions build up. But because you don't know how to express emotion, you get mad.

Get inside your own head today. This is going to take some time, so set a timer for ten minutes and really think about it. If you're an Enneagram Three like me, this is not a normal exercise for you! But if I did it, so can you. Set a timer and get a notebook to brain stream your thoughts.

Today's verse is important to our journey with affection. It has to do with **fear**. Write it on your hand or post it where you can see it today!

"For God gave us a spirit not of fear but of power and love and self-control."
-2 Timothy 1:7

CHAPTER THREE

PERFECT LOVE CASTS OUT FEAR

I want you to think of your heart as a house. It's a beautiful house, one that's been well cared for over the years. Then one day a visitor stops by: A pretty nasty dude, always nagging about things that might happen. He brings up worries over the future: "what-ifs" and "what-thens." He was supposed to visit, but he ends up staying. He sets up shop in the guest room. Pretty soon his stuff is spilling into every room in the beautiful house – ugly stuff, remnants from a past he can't let go. He doesn't like sunlight, so he draws all the blinds. The house starts to become dark and dusty. He hates visitors because he hates new things, so he locks the front door to keep community away.

That visitor is Fear. When you let him in the door of your heart, you're letting him in to stay. Pretty soon he'll invite his friends Anxiety, Depression, and Isolation, and they'll stay too. Pride and Gracelessness will join him, and Control isn't far behind. The house will be full, but it will be dark and crowded. There's no room for light and freedom.

Now imagine that the Landlord of the house stops by to see why the blinds have been drawn so long. He unlocks the door, takes one look around, and seizes Fear by the collar. "You don't belong here!" He states firmly. "I'm evicting you from the premises." And he takes Fear, his friends, and all his ugly stuff and *casts him out of the house.*

Sometimes I need an image of what God does for us through His Spirit. This analogy sums up what John described when He said, "There is no fear in love, but perfect love casts out fear. For fear has to do with punishment, and whoever fears has not been perfected in love." (1 John 4:18) God is the **epitome** of love; perfect love. When you invite Him into the core of your being, into the darkest and most broken parts of you, He literally *casts out fear.* He takes it by the collar and throws it in the street! Fear cannot live in the same space as the Spirit of God.

The key here is *knowing* the love of God, which you do

by being in the Word. If you're struggling with affection, I recommend being **daily** in the Word. This devotional should not be replacing your time in Scripture. I will be very disappointed if it does! Start somewhere simple, like John or Psalms, get a notebook, and write down what you observe about God. Then write down how this changes the way you live. This will teach you *knowledge* of God's love, which leads to the second step: *Believing* God's love. Believing God actually loves you and that His love changes your life is like inviting the Landlord into the house. Fear can't be kicked out until Perfect Love walks in.

Today, assess your spiritual life. Have you been in the Word? Yes or no? Why or why not? How can you change this? Don't shut this book until you've answered that question!

You cannot change how you act in your marriage and relationships unless you are walking with God, and you can't walk with God apart from His Word and Spirit. Your verse for today should remind you of this!

> *"And this is love, that we walk according to his commandments; this is the commandment, just as you have heard from the beginning, so that you should walk in it."*
> -2 John 1:6

CHAPTER FOUR

YOU ARE NOT ENOUGH ON YOUR OWN

Everywhere I look these days there's a quote saying, "You are enough." Obviously this is something we need to hear or it wouldn't resonate so much. Yet, from a biblical perspective this isn't completely true!

Apart from Jesus, we fall hopelessly short in life and godliness. If you don't like hearing that, think about why you're reading this book. Have you not fallen short in the affection category? Do you see this as a problem? I know I do! I am not "enough" for the people I love when I try to love them in my own power, and neither are you.

It's a tough message, one we don't like to hear. Some people say it's discouraging. But it's only discouraging when you hear the first half. The second half is altogether *empowering*.

Yes, on our own strength, we aren't enough. We fall short. We mess up. We start over. But Jesus didn't die for us to live in defeat. He died to provide us with a way to *abundance*. He didn't mean gorgeous cars and expensive houses, but an abundance of spiritual *strength*. Jesus provided a way to live on a higher plane, to live in *super*natural strength. Supernatural literally means *beyond our natural ability*.

RIght now, giving affection is beyond your natural ability. So to overcome this area of your life, you need *supernatural strength and love*. This is what Jesus provides for you! Where you are not enough, He is your enoughness. He fills in the gaps for you. The Holy Spirit, your Helper, does this for you as you walk in step with Him.

So how do you embrace this enough-ness and let the Spirit lead you into strength? Once again, it starts with the Word (get used to hearing that!). Being in the Word exposes you to God's truth and love, which the Spirit reminds you about throughout the day. Secondly, prayer is vital to owning your identity in Christ. I don't mean 20 minutes on your knees every morning. I mean daily, hourly, moment by moment dependence on God through prayer! Most of my prayers happen at my stove, while I'm walking, as I'm rocking a baby or doing some task. In moments when I am especially overwhelmed – such as when I feel overcome by anger, fear, or my inability to let down emotional walls – I pour myself out to God.

Sometimes I do this out loud. Sometimes I go in my room for a few minutes. Sometimes I write it out. But One thing I frequently say: "Lord, I know you promise your Spirit to make me enough in this area. I'm not leaving, I'm not ceasing to pray until you come through for your promise." This kind of bold prayer is foreign to many Christians. They are not taught to call upon God for His promises, but that's exactly what He wants you to do!

Today, be conscious of how often you pray. Do you revert to worry instead of prayer? Take those moments and turn them into conversations with God. Don't "fix" your prayers. Pour them out. That's what He wants.

"Do not be anxious about anything, but in everything by prayer and supplication with thanksgiving let your requests be made known to God."
-Phil. 4:6

CHAPTER FIVE

AFRAID OF FAILING

Josh walked in the door – I heard it creak on its hinges – and I scrunched my eyes by the stove around the corner. *You can do it. It's one simple step.*

I smiled as I greeted him and, in a step that took everything in me, I hugged him closely and kissed him hello.

If someone could have read my thoughts in that moment, there would have been dozens of voices to record:

What kind of wife are you that this is so difficult?
Look how stupid you look!
Why should you be making this effort? It's not your love

language.

He'll notice that you did this and it will be awkward – you never initiate affection.

So many voices. So much condemnation. So much... *fear.* I was afraid of failing at affection because it is so unnatural to me...so uncomfortable and awkward. I was convinced that the smallest effort would come off as strange, even repulsive, to my husband. Even though I took action, my head was still in a very negative place.

Do you fear failing? Do you fear being bad at loving your husband, kids, and friends? You're not alone. It's why we don't try. We're scared of either being rejected or looking stupid or simply doing affection badly. Can I offer you a freeing thought?

People don't usually care *how* love is expressed to them. They just appreciate that you expressed it, imperfectly though it may be. Your husband might comment on your effort, but he's probably not judging how you hugged! Your kids might laugh that you kissed them when you never do, but over time, they'll stop commenting. And one day they'll be glad you did.

Fear holds us back from making an effort. It tells us that failure is inevitable, without ever defining what failure is. Is it starting and stopping? Hugging stiffly? Being someone you're "not?" Identify the fear. What are you **really** afraid of? Losing control, saving face? Afraid of losing someone close to you? Afraid of being exposed or looking silly? I have struggled with all of these, but the key to breaking free in this area of life is to **identify** the fear and commit it to the One who made you.

He did not make you to be in bondage to anything, including your own inhibitions and fears.

"There is no fear in love. But perfect love drives out fear, because fear has to do with punishment. The one who fears is not made perfect in love."
-1 John 4:8

CHAPTER SIX

BROKENNESS ON DISPLAY

My friends know I am working through this affection thing. One friend in particular has made a game of "rating" my hugs, noting how much I have improved each time. With these people, I am comfortable talking about my struggle, and they are close enough to me to lovingly joke about it!

But sometimes strangers notice that I'm uncomfortable being affectionate, even though I try to go through the socially acceptable means of greeting. In these moments I feel like my weakness is on display for everyone to see. Or when I'm out with my husband and I see other couples, with wives who naturally want to be close, and that old condemnation creeps into my mind:

Why can't you be like that?

Not good enough. Not sweet enough. Not loving enough.

When my brokenness is on display, to myself or to others, I am faced with a choice. You, too, are faced with a choice: To listen to the voice of condemnation, or to **stop**, redirect, and listen to the voice of Christ.

Romans 8 tells us that there is **no** condemnation for those who are under the name and sacrifice of Christ Jesus. At the end of that same chapter Paul informs us that what Jesus did makes us **more** than conquerors in Christ: **more** than the Roman conquerors of old, who have gone down in history as the best of the best. In Christ, we are better at conquering than the Romans! We are overcomers in absolutely every sense.

When my broken, weak self is displayed for everyone to observe is when I tap into the power of God through His Holy Spirit. In the moment when the lies start spilling into my mind I surrender them to the wisdom and truth of God. I invite Him into my thoughts, asking for His truth to replace the untruth, and I verbally reject the lies.

Preaching truth to yourself when the lies come in is the most effective way to fight back. If you hold onto those thoughts, dwell on them, sit with them – you **will** become like them. But you don't have to. Your brokenness is not your identity. Your brokenness was taken over by God, consumed by the fire of His grace, and made glorious in Christ. **his** brokenness was put on display so yours could bear you no shame.

So hold your husband's hand, dear girl. Those lies have no power over you.

"That is why we labor and strive, because we have put our hope in the living God, who is the Savior of all people, and especially of those who believe."
-1 Tim. 4:10

CHAPTER SEVEN
NURTURING LITTLE LOVES

Perhaps the most terrifying thought as a woman who struggles with affection is the impact it will have on my kids. I love my girls with everything I have, but the way I naturally show love isn't something they would recognize at ages three and one. And as they get older, their need to be embraced and kissed won't fade. Children need affection, and yet I struggle to give it to them.

I think the sheer demand of affection on the woman who doesn't like it makes this journey very overwhelming at first. I felt so ill equipped, so condemned, and so incapable of providing what my family needed. Even trying to give a huge felt like a herculean effort.

How was I supposed to do this day after day?

God was doing a work in my heart spiritually and emotionally, but alongside Him, I had to take a step of faith. I had to believe that He was doing a good work that He planned to finish, and that my job in the meantime was to give to my babies what they needed most. I had to step out, step up, and *act how I wanted to feel.*

This is not fake. It's faith. It's faith that God is doing the spiritual work and that we're living up to the work He is doing. It's dependence on His strength and obedience to His call. If we wait to **feel** like embracing our little ones, or if we let **fear** hold us back, we will not nurture the little loves who, through our example, are being taught what love looks like.

Because the alternative is to repeat the pattern. It's to withhold ourselves from our kids until the "right" time, when we **feel** capable, even as time slips away. Even as they grow up. Even as we miss opportunity after opportunity because we were too wrapped up in shame to live as overcomers.

Each time we place faith in God's work and take action based on obedience (not emotion) we're fighting back against the enemy's attack on our family. He **wants** your kids to repeat your weakness.

He wants your daughter telling her college roommate how she felt unloved as a child and isn't great at affection because of it (sound familiar?).

> The pattern stops with **us**.
> The pattern stops with **God**.
> The pattern stops **today**.

> *"Who shall separate us from the love of Christ? Shall trouble or hardship or persecution or famine or nakedness or danger or sword? As it is written: 'For your sake we face death all day long; we are considered as sheep to be slaughtered.' No, in all these things we are more than conquerors through him who loved us."*
> –Romans 8:35-37

CHAPTER EIGHT

PRESSING THROUGH SHAME

Shame is a weight. It sits heavy on our shoulders, weighing us down as we walk out God's call on our lives. We wonder why following Jesus feels like such a drag: Because we're dragging all this baggage around with us! There He is, the Messiah, offering to take it if we would "cast all our cares," but we hang onto it. "No, Lord!" We say through our thoughts and actions. "It's mine! I'll carry it!"
Nevermind that we can't accomplish what He wants us to do with our hands full of shame.

Jesus was sent to give victory over sin, death, and the devil. He did this through the cross and resurrection!

We can say "**amazing grace**!" because His sacrifice paid the debt we owed to God. We know all this in theory... but do we know it in reality? Do we **live** as if it is true, particularly when it comes to affection?

If we believe shameful things about ourselves, owning shame as part of our identity, we will not be free. It's that simple. The key to freedom is pressing *through* shame to the Savior on the other side. The Savior who defeated death, who conquered shame, so we would no longer bear it. Jesus – what a beautiful name indeed!

If you're still living under a burden of shame, my question for you is: Have you surrendered your past failures to the Lord? Have you brought them to the cross – and *left them there?*

Victory is not linear, but it's also not found in picking up what was cast down. If you want to overcome this struggle and really address the fears holding you back, you **must** surrender your shame. Letting go of shame feels like wearing new clothes: Like something is missing, slightly uncomfortable even. And it **should** feel like something is missing because something **is** missing: **condemnation**!

Shame is not your master, and you are not shame's slave. You do not have to listen or obey that voice. When shame comes to you, saying:

"You'll never be enough for your husband/kids/

community."

"You'll never be able to love them physically."

"You'll never get over the lack of affection your parents showed you."

You have a choice: Shove those lies right back in the Enemy's face, or act as if they are true.

Which will you choose?

> *"Fear not, for you will not be ashamed; be not confounded, for you will not be disgraced; for you will forget the shame of your youth, and the reproach of your widowhood you will remember no more."*
> -Isaiah 54:4

CHAPTER NINE
I NEED TO FEEL SAFE

It was during our first married fight - the real kind, not the cute, cleaned-up, honeymoon kind - that I realized how big a role fear played in my life. I was in the corner of our kitchen, arms crossed, anger boiling, with a husband who didn't seem to understand me at all.

"You only seem to have one emotion," he said. "Anger."

That's when I said, without thinking, "I'm angry because I'm afraid *I'm not enough.*"

And then I cried. Because I had never actually articulated why anger was my go-to emotion, the safest one with which I'd engage. Anger was familiar, and it protected me from the vulnerability and weakness of other feelings, like affection or love. I was angry because I felt I had to prove myself, then angry that in proving myself, I **still** wasn't enough. I could be anything - I could achieve almost anything - and yet here I was, still failing, because my only emotion was anger.

As time went by I came to see that conversation as a peek inside my own soul. If you're not a very introspective person, analyzing yourself isn't high on your list of to-do's. But take the time to evaluate **why** you act the way you do and **why** you are averse to affection. This is key to overcoming in this struggle. And often, our aversion to affection is because we feel either "not enough" or "unsafe."

I want to clarify: Josh himself **never** made me feel unsafe, emotionally or otherwise. I have *always* felt that emotions are unsafe because people don't appreciate them. People *reject*. And for many years I believed there was nothing weaker - or harder to respect - than an emotion-driven person. So between fear of being unsafe, and my need to maintain a respectable persona, emotions (and thus, affection) were sidelined.

Do you react in anger because feeling something seems unsafe? Are you scared of opening up because you think it won't be well-received? So much of our struggle with affection begins here! These fears are often rooted in our childhood wounds - an over-critical parent who didn't care about emotions, being bullied and name-called in school, or being abused by people who should have loved you. Overcoming these wounds is not a quick process and I recommend counseling from someone who is biblically based to help you on that journey. As you begin these steps to freedom, remember that fear has no hold on us in Christ. Even when humans are completely "unsafe" for our emotions, we can trust that God **sees** and **knows** our hearts. Safety is found in Him.

My marriage wasn't fixed overnight with that kitchen confession. In fact, our marriage got **worse** before it got better. But I learned that I couldn't expect my husband to fulfill me emotionally, and I couldn't put him in the place of God. I started processing my emotions with the Lord **first**, and that changed how I interacted with Josh. Five years in, our marriage truly has been healed in this area. We are so much stronger, closer, and happier than in that first year. But it's not because of me or Josh; it's because of Jesus.

If you want to feel safe emotionally, start with the safest Person you know: God Himself.

> *"The Lord is my light and my salvation—whom shall I fear? The Lord is the stronghold of my life— of whom shall I be afraid?"*

CHAPTER TEN

WHAT IF I'M REJECTED?

-Psalm 27:1

What if I step out, reach out, put myself out there...and I'm rejected?

That's the root of it all, really. Fear of rejection.

I once heard someone say our fear of what **could** happen is usually worse than what actually does occur. But to overcome it we have to think about the worse case scenario: What if the worst happens? What if we **do** get rejected? *So what?*

When I think about the sinking feeling of someone pulling away, or the sting of not being received, it's enough to set me back **years** in this affection journey. But then I think about risks versus rewards: I can live in slavery to what "could" happen, or I can step out and obey God, even in my weakness. If rejection happens... it happens. I can't control the outcome. But I can control myself.

We have to be willing to say, "So what? So what if I am rejected by people? I am accepted and embraced by God!" Christ died to make us acceptable when we couldn't do so for ourselves. Friends - read that again. *He died to make you acceptable.* Is there any person in this world who gave up that much for you? Any person whose rejection could matter more than Christ's acceptance?

Let's not let fear of **people** blind us to the love of God. When we elevate the rejection of man, we're in danger of demeaning Jesus' sacrifice. That's a weighty thought.

Practically speaking, this battle will play out in a matter of seconds. The instant you feel the fear of rejection, you have to be ready to preach truth to your heart. You need to become hyper aware of your thought patterns and responses, because that's where the battle is fought. Old habits die hard. Jesus saves us, but we have to choose to live under His influence! Freedom is a fight.

Paul told us if we walk by the Spirit, we won't gratify the desires of the flesh (Gal. 5:16). We won't give into fear of man, fear of rejection, or old emotional patterns **if** we stop and agree with the Spirit of God in us. It's being still enough to hear the whisper: "You are accepted in Me." It's stopping yourself before you withdraw to emotional "safety" (read: slavery) and choosing to trust God's love for you. It's stepping forward in courage that God is present with you, even when showing affection demands everything of you.

I like to think of giving affection as a slap in the enemy's face. Every time I believe God's words to me and step into that place of strength, I'm shaking off the emotional chains with which the enemy has tried to bind me. I'm believing God. I'm choosing courage.

I might get rejected. So what?

> *"So I say, walk by the Spirit, and you will not gratify the desires of the flesh."*
> -Galatians 5:16

CHAPTER ELEVEN

I'M FAILING AT MARRIAGE

This is for the girl who feels like she's not enough for her husband.

I see you. I've been you.

Maybe your husband, like mine, is a physical-touch love language. And you're over here in the corner thinking, *I'm fine if I never touch anyone, ever.*

It's hard! You want him to know you love him, but you don't express love through hugs and kisses. Or maybe you used to, when you were dating. When you had strict physical standards and those things were all you could do. But then you got married and sex was on the table, so affection went out the window. And now he feels tricked and you feel like a loser.

Do you relate?

Hear me, friend: God wants a beautiful, intimate relationship for you and your husband. He wants you to be fulfilled by Him and by one another. He wants to see you full of joy and closeness, no longer miscommunicating but communicating **well**. He is a God of unity and true love! But God also knows that you are fallen, and your husband is fallen, and sanctification is a process. Your husband needs to have patience. You need grace and courage. God is able to provide both.

I could give you more advice but I'm going to share the one thing that transformed everything for us: Pray. I'm serious. Every time you feel desperate or unequipped, pray. Pray for your husband. Pray for yourself. Pray for your marriage. There is a spiritual battle against your marriage because your marriage depicts the gospel, all the more because you follow Christ. Why **wouldn't** the enemy attack you? Why **wouldn't** the enemy want a wedge between you and your spouse? You're in a battle whether you like it or not. So pray like you are.

You might feel like you're failing at marriage, but I promise you this: If you are in Christ and fighting for your marriage in prayer, you are not failing. You're winning. You're winning because you're on the winning side; with a victorious God who fights the battle on your behalf. But you have to stop doing it on **your** strength and instead seek **his**. Prayer is your way of acknowledging that you need God. It's your invitation for Him to come in power.

Take five minutes right now, set a timer, and pray for your spouse and your marriage (if you're single, pray over your future relationship!).

"And if we know that he hears us—whatever we ask—we know that we have what we asked of him."
-1 John 5:15

CHAPTER TWELVE
ACTION PRECEDES EMOTION

When teaching on Bible study, I frequently tell women they won't always FEEL like drawing near to God through His Word. But "feeling' is not our measure of what we should do! In our walk with God, obedience often precedes positive emotions. Our feelings change as we walk in trust by obeying God.

This principle has carried over in my journey with intimacy. If I wait to **feel** like giving affection, it just won't happen. It's always a little uncomfortable for me (sometimes **very** uncomfortable), so giving affection is a choice. It's a choice to take the step of showing love to those close to me even before I feel like it.

Now, clearly, I am not talking about giving affection to abusive or manipulative people. And I am certainly not talking about giving of yourself sexually to someone who demands it (including your husband! Sex is to be mutual). This section applies to generally healthy marriages and women who are averse to affection and don't often think of or feel like physically showing love.

Gretchen Rubin, an expert on habits and human nature, frequently advises people who struggle with changing their behavior to "Act how you want to feel." If you want to be more energetic, get up and do something active! Don't wait until you **feel** more active to get up and move, because it probably won't happen. The same can be applied to affection. As you work through the spiritual aspect with the Lord, you will have opportunities to show affection. If you wait to feel like hugging your friend or kissing your husband, it probably won't happen. Instead, step through the discomfort and just do it. See how you feel afterward. Analyze your emotions: Do you feel relieved? Anxious? Worried over their response to you? Deal with the emotions after the fact, but do not let them dictate your actions **before** you take them.

For me, showing affection to my family has been a step of faith in God's provision. God says He will strengthen me and help me (Psalm 73), but I can only know that strength and help if I step out in obedience. Some days, this is very difficult for me! But the more I step out in faith, not feeling, the easier it becomes and the more I see God's hand moving in my life.

My challenge for you today: Think about how often you let your feelings, not faith, dictate your actions. This applies to all areas, not just affection!

"For the righteousness of God is revealed from faith for faith, as it is written, 'The righteous shall live by faith.'"
-Romans 1:17

CHAPTER THIRTEEN
AFFECTION IS NOT WEAKNESS

Oh, how this chapter hits home.

For years I saw affection and emotion as "weak." I had very little respect for emotional people, and would shut down in conversation as soon as I perceived what I deemed "weakness." And because I didn't respect affection or emotion in other people, I certainly didn't show it myself. As I shared earlier in this devotional, my husband finally told me: "You only have one emotion... anger."

Anger was my primary emotion because anger meant strength. Anger meant power and control. But in my heart I felt very *out of control.* I was scared of showing positive or sensitive emotions because this meant being vulnerable; it meant risking rejection. My anger was just a way of dealing with how unsafe I felt.

Changing our mentality toward affection is key to changing our behavior. Romans 12:1-2 tells us we cannot be transformed if our minds are not renewed. Changed behavior requires changed minds. So what lies do we believe about affection? What lies do we believe about emotional intimacy?

A few lies I've believed:

- Affection and emotion are for people who are mentally and emotionally weak.
- Giving affection means giving up control and opening myself up to hurt.
- I will always be rejected if I initiate affection.
- I am not capable of changing.
- Withholding affection/being emotionally unavailable is just part of who I am.

What lies do you believe? Take a moment to write them down.

Sometimes the lies we believe are rooted in past abuse. If you have been abused, I recommend finding a biblical counselor to work with. This book will not be enough to set you on a path of healing!

Other times the lies we believe come from childhood

wounds: Unavailable or angry parents, rejection from dear friends, or high school break ups. We unknowingly allow those hurts to dictate how we act in future relationships.

I always come back to the power of Christ through the gospel to heal us and make us whole. Jesus died to reconcile us to Him and show us what true love looks like. He also said that we would experience suffering in this world, but to "take heart! I have overcome the world." (John 16:33) If He is sufficient to overcome the world, He is sufficient to overcome the hurting places of our past. He is sufficient to change how we think about affection and intimacy. He can transform us through renewed minds!

Right now, commit the lies you have believed about yourself, about affection, and about emotional intimacy to God. Give them to Jesus and invite His sufficiency into your broken places. Allow Him to speak truth to you through His Word.

"We demolish arguments and every pretension that sets itself up against the knowledge of God, and we take captive every thought to make it obedient to Christ."
-2 Corinthians 10:5

CHAPTER FOURTEEN

PERSONALITY IS NOT AN EXCUSE

Are you into the Enneagram? Or maybe Myers Briggs? Both these personality tests have been immensely helpful to me and my marriage. I am an Enneagram three and an ENTJ on MBTI. ENTJ stands for "extroverted intuitive thinking judging" - also known as the Achiever. It's very easy for me to disengage emotionally to get a job done.

My personality type is known for being emotionally unavailable. We don't "do" feelings. But just because a test tells me this is "normal" for people who think like me doesn't mean I should stay that way.

These tests are popular and helpful, but as Christians, there's an element of growth we cannot ignore. For us, personality is progressive. We should be growing and changing as Jesus sanctifies us through the Holy Spirit. This means the Phylicia of today should not be the same person as the Phylicia of next year, at least in regard to sinful or fear-based behaviors.

If we want to make progress in affection and emotional intimacy, we have to stop making excuses for ourselves. Yes, our personalities affect how we see the world and interact with others. But they are not a box we are destined to remain inside for life. And the more we focus inward, celebrating our personality instead of celebrating the good work God's Spirit is doing in us, the less we can give *outward*. And the Great Commission Jesus gave us in Matthew 28:20 is an *outward* call.

Knowing oneself may help you love others more effectively, but only if that knowledge draws you to the throne of grace. Transformation will happen only if your knowledge of yourself keeps Jesus on the throne and motivates you to obey Him. Be careful not to get caught in an endless trap of personality worship: Fixing your eyes on who you want to be or who a test says you are, instead of on who Jesus wants you to become.

Instead, use what you learn about your personality to take note of your weak points. Take note when you find yourself falling back into old patterns and habits. Troubleshoot those patterns with daily habits of showing love and affection, even though it may not come naturally to you. Be that rare individual who uses personality, not as a means to celebrate who you already are, but as a launching pad to the person God wants you to be.

> "...being confident of this, that he who began a good work in you will carry it on to completion until the day of Christ Jesus."
> -Philippians 1:6

CHAPTER FIFTEEN

ACKNOWLEDGING YOUR OWN EMOTIONS

My sisters are extremely musical. Not only are they talented musicians, they also listen to music on a regular basis. I, on the other hand, do not.

Sure, I have a few playlists I'll turn on when I'm focused on work. I have some favorite CDs in my car. But music is not something I listen to regularly; I tend to lean toward podcasts at 1.5 speed!

I didn't think much of it until my sisters discovered just how little I listen to music. Aghast, they asked **why** I didn't listen to it as often as they did. I hadn't thought about it until they asked, and as the words came out of my mouth I had a realization: I don't listen to music because it brings up too many emotions, and emotions slow me down.

Happy music might motivate me for a bit, but when a slow or nostalgic song comes on, I'm immediately back in 2008 driving my red PT Cruiser post-high school and then I'm tearing up at some memory and suddenly not getting anything done (this may be my Enneagram Four wing coming out!)! Since my time is so limited with two small kids, I just can't afford to get too much in my own head. Music tends to be more of a distraction for me than anything else, so I limit how much I play it.

Why do I share all this? It's certainly not to dictate how much you listen to music! It's to point out that our relationship to our **emotions** has a greater effect on daily life than we think. Music triggers something in me emotionally. When my emotions are triggered, I can't focus on the tasks at hand. When I was in an unhealthy place, those emotional triggers made me intensely uncomfortable. I would either keep the music on to dwell in the feeling, or I would shut it off and stuff the feelings away.

We are not meant to live for our emotions, from high to high or low to low. But we are also not meant to ignore them, because God gave them to us! I'm learning to acknowledge and appreciate what I am feeling, which is hard to do since I spent so many years locking my feelings away. Allowing myself to feel is a conscious effort, and it may be a conscious effort for you as well. If you get uncomfortable with emotions that rise up, however they are triggered, take a moment to *acknowledge the feeling*. Identify it. Be real with it. Then give it to the Lord. I don't always shut off the music when I practice this; sometimes it's just what I need for that moment. But sometimes I can sense that dwelling on the emotion too long isn't going to serve me well, so I give it to the Lord and move on with my responsibilities.

Acknowledging your emotions is a big part of growing spiritually. I love how the Psalms incorporate emotion and music into worship of God! In fact, I would encourage you to read in Psalms today in your Bible study. Psalm 118 is one of my favorites.

> "In my anguish I cried to the Lord; He answered me by setting me free."
> –Psalm 118:5

CHAPTER SIXTEEN

AFFECTION AFTER WOUNDING

For many of us, our fear of giving or receiving affection is rooted in a past wound. We trusted someone enough to let them in, they hurt us, and now the walls are up. How do we grow in showing affection, being open to love, when we've been wounded in the past?

Remember the Enneagram, a personality framework that has recently become popular? One of the core principles of Enneagram has to do with our childhood wound. Who we are as people, the Enneagram teaches, is linked to something we experienced as a child. Whatever wound we received now drives our motives and behaviors. For someone like me – a Three – that wound may have been rejection by my peers or a critical authority figure. Even if I wasn't abused, the impact of those experiences affected my mind and heart, and affects how I look at the world even today.

The Enneagram is helpful for understanding ourselves and others, but if it is divorced from the gospel, it can give us no hope for real healing. And without real healing, we can't live an overcoming life in the area of affection. I don't know about you, but I don't want to live my entire life captive to childhood wounds! I want to steadily grow to a greater understanding of who God is and how He heals even the deepest hurts of my past. I am sure you want the same.

Fortunately for us, God doesn't call us to "just move on" from the wounds we've experienced. He doesn't call us to ignore them, stuff them away, or pretend they don't affect us. But He **does** call us to cast them on Him (1 Peter 5:7). That verse actually says, 'Cast all your anxieties on Him, because He cares for you.' So few people actually practice this! We live in an age of anxiety, and while there is much more treating anxiety than "just praying about it," I think we'd see much less captivity in this area if people actually practiced what Peter said. Personally, as I have grown in affection and my understanding of it, I have had to cast my anxieties on God as often as every *hour*. That's exactly what Peter is talking about. Nowhere in Scripture does God say overcoming our fears, worries, and wounds is a one-time thing. This is a daily walk, a continual relationship, an hour-by-hour overcoming.

I always recommend finding a biblical counselor to process your past wounds. I also recommend (and so does Scripture!) connecting to a strong, biblical church community as you grow in this area. Connect with godly people, and learn to be vulnerable with them. This, coupled with the growth of your prayer life and daily "casting of cares," will help you process the wounds of the past so you can walk free in the future.

> *"Cast all your anxieties on Him, because He cares for you."*
> -1 Peter 5:7

CHAPTER SEVENTEEN

ACCEPTING GRACE FOR YOUR WEAKNESS

The struggles of our life - external and internal - expose our weakness. Perhaps that's one reason we resist them so much! No one likes to have their weakness exposed.

I must remind myself almost daily that it is my *weakness* that magnifies God's grace. My weakness makes God's greatness so much more visible, both to myself and to others. But acknowledging my weak areas requires another step: Accepting this grace God offers.

Isn't it wild that the simple step of acceptance is *so hard?* We know God's grace in theory; we know He loves us according to the Word; we know He is sufficient for our weakness. But when push comes to shove, we simply refuse to embrace the grace He offers. Our reluctance to actually *believe* and *trust* God's grace results in double-minded lives. We struggle with guilt and doubt and shame because we don't feel "worthy" to accept God's grace.

Want to hear something freeing? You're not worthy of God's grace. *That's why it's called grace.*

This concept was so difficult for me to wrap my mind around, it took **years** for me to really see grace for what it is: The unmerited favor of God. "Unmerited" means you can't earn it. It's freely given (more on this in a forthcoming chapter!). Pretending it wasn't given to you, or letting it sit there unopened because you "feel bad" for the gift, will keep you perpetually beholden to guilt and shame. But the people who actually **open** and **enjoy** the gift? They're the ones overwhelmed by joy!

We can have overflowing joy in the middle of this affection journey simply by accepting God's grace toward us. Reject the lies and distractions the enemy throws at you, and *believe God* when He says He loves you, He defends you, and He is sufficient for your weakness. God has known about your weakness from the beginning; confession is just how we, as humans, humbly stay in relationship with Him. If He knew and offered grace anyway, what are you achieving by refusing to accept it?

Today, ask God to help you receive, embrace, and enjoy His gift of grace. Spend five minutes right now (set a timer) to think about the grace He has given. How would life change if you accepted that He loves you, and that His favor is on you?

"Do not grieve, for the joy of the Lord is your strength."
-Nehemiah 8:10

CHAPTER EIGHTEEN

SPEAKING A LOVE LANGUAGE YOU DON'T KNOW

Almost every couple deals with differing sexual drives, whether all the time or on occasion. Through most of our marriage, I have been the higher drive spouse. At times, I was frustrated that Josh didn't seem interested after what I deemed an extensive amount of time! I asked him **how** he could *possibly* be such a camel when it came to the sexual side of our relationship!

Josh explained that for him, lack of affection translates to lack of intimacy overall. If there wasn't any lead-up throughout the day, no physical interaction or touch of any kind, he wasn't in the mood or even **thinking** about sex in the evening - the old "sex begins in the kitchen" adage. And I was the opposite - I don't need affection to be engaged sexually because sex and affection are not connected in my mind (they should be, but they're not unless I make a concerted effort).

This is the crazy cycle into which so many of us fall. For some of you, your husband is the higher drive spouse. But I've noticed a pattern with a lot of women who struggle with affection - they, too, are eager to participate in sex, but withhold themselves from affection. Giving physical touch to their spouse outside of the bedroom requires dismantling the box they've created in their minds. It requires speaking a love language in which they are not fluent.

When we took the love language test, I got a **zero** for physical touch. An actual **zero**. As I've shared before, hugging, kissing, patting someone's back or doing anything more than a high-five with adults *doesn't even cross my mind.* Josh, of course, got something like an eight or a nine out of ten for physical touch. Ah, God is so funny. In order for our relationship to work, Josh has to give me grace for growth. He frequently shows love to me via **my** love languages, but even when he does, it doesn't trigger a physical touch response from me. That's not how this works! Rather, I must be absolutely intentional about showing love to him physically. I have to actually write it down, prioritize it, even keep it on my daily list. At one point, I had "kiss Josh" on my list of daily habits!

I believe how I am wired can be overcome by the Spirit of God when I follow His plan for my relationship. I'm not doing this perfectly, but I **am** trying to walk by the Spirit using the love language my husband best understands. It's really hard sometimes, and we still fall into the crazy cycle. But I'm making an effort to learn the language. Are you?

If you haven't checked out *The Five Love Languages*, you can get the book on Amazon, at your library, or on their website. There is also a free languages quiz on their site.

> *"Whoever lives in love lives in God, and God in them."*
> -Ephesians 4:2

CHAPTER NINETEEN

FAILURE IS NOT THE END

During the months that I wrote this little book, Josh and I had many conversations about my own journey with affection. As these words were typed for you to read, I struggled deeply with showing love to Josh physically. It doesn't take more than two days for me to fall out of the habit of affection, and that has occurred multiple times. I have failed in showing love this way.

But something I learned in my journey through sexual sin applies just as much here: Victory is a lifestyle, not a destination. We don't get to a plateau of spiritual growth and just "get over" those besetting struggles of our flesh. Jesus told us He offers abundant, overcoming life, but He didn't say it would all happen in one day. To the contrary, we have to walk in step with Him *every day* to see consistent victory.

Dear friend, you will fail in this journey. You will fail the expectations and hopes you had for yourself. That failure is not the end of things; it's evidence of trying. It's evidence of growth. What matters is not that you failed; it's what you *do* with your failure. We can wallow in our inabilities, find people to sympathize and talk to us about our struggles, or throw a pity party for ourselves. Or we can take our struggle to the Lord, reconcile and communicate to our loved ones, and try again the next day. The Holy Spirit is our Helper and our Comforter. He not only enables us to victory, He comforts us when we repent after failure!

You might make a lot of progress in this month of reading these little devotions, but next month find yourself retreating back into yourself and your past. In that moment, you have a choice: Focus on your own failure, your own inability, or turn to the One who enables you in the first place! We are not doing this on our own strength. **clearly** our own strength has not worked in the past. When we fail to love our dear ones with the affection they need, we get a chance to start over the next day, hour or even minute.

Have hope, my friend. It's not over. Every hour is a new chance to walk by the Spirit. He will strengthen and enable you to do the good work He has called you to do.

> *"He will strengthen you, help you, uphold you with His righteous right hand."*
> -Isaiah 41:10

CHAPTER TWENTY

THE SEX-LOVE CONNECTION

Alright. We're going there. It's time to talk about the connection between love - intimate, emotional love - and the bedroom.

Would it shock you to know the first time I said "I love you" during sex was *four years* into my marriage?

It took me that long to connect my emotions to the sexual act. I was perfectly okay with being physically naked with my husband, but I could not bare my soul. I could not let myself *feel* because it was scarier to have a naked heart than it was to have a naked body.

It's sad, I know. But spiritual growth, and relational

growth, is slow. Rather than list all the ways we wish we weren't like this, we should celebrate the little steps we take to grow in understanding. For me, understanding the sex-love connection - and recognizing just how stunted I was in that area - helped me see my need for Christ's regeneration.

Sometimes sex is easier than love. Love requires vulnerability, commitment, sacrifice, and spiritual nakedness. Love requires looking at a person's ugliness and giving them your best - at least according to biblical love (1 Corinthians 13).In my marriage, I feared Josh seeing my real self and walking away. The rejection of guys I liked in high school, the rejection of girls who didn't want to be my friend, and the rejection of people close to me caught up to me. Marriage exposed me. I saw it this way: Every day I was supposed to draw emotionally closer to this man I married, but every day he drew near, the more stifled I felt. Having someone that close, that often, wasn't my comfort zone. I didn't want it in daily life and I certainly didn't want it in the bedroom.

As a Christian, I knew all the facts about sex being an intimate act, and I believed sex to be absolutely sacred. I knew the consequences of sexual sin. But in my own marriage experiencing real intimacy - emotionally, not just physically - evaded me. I never brought my whole self to the bedroom, just my body. I was too scared to connect sex and love.

This is the great dichotomy of intimacy: In order to experience its fullness, we must risk its loss. In order to have the richness of emotional-physical love, we have to bring our whole selves to the sexual relationship. That is terrifying to someone who struggles with rejection.

Overcoming this is a daily journey for me, and it will be so for you as well. Your first step is to keep rebuking fear through your faith in God. Your next step is to keep showing up to meet the Lord so He can fight your fear-battles for you. And your third step is to bring your whole self - risks and all - to your marriage bed (current or future).

I'm right here with you. I don't know if I've said I love you in the bedroom lately. It's not natural for me. So I'm here with you as you learn to open yourself up to your spouse, or if you're single, prepare your heart to one day be vulnerable with him. Remember that God's work in you is slow work; don't give up too soon. He's the one changing you! Your responsibility? To keep walking closer to Him as He does.

> "A man leaves his father and mother and is united to his wife, and they become one flesh."
> –Genesis 2:24

CHAPTER TWENTY ONE

BREAKING THE HOLD OF INSECURITY

I remember the very first time I felt insecure. I walked into my kindergarten classroom and saw all the other little girls in their dresses and bows (this was, after all, the nineties). Immediately I wondered, "Am I as pretty as they are?" I spent most of that year trying to fit in and keep up. My parents noticed this, and after deliberating, pulled me out of school and homeschooled me for first grade. What started as a one-year experiment ended with me being homeschooled through my high school graduation!

My parents' decision played a big part in who I am today. In the school environment, I don't think my leadership skills would have grown the way they did in the freedom of home education. I needed personalized attention and a peer-pressure-free environment to step into the leader I actually am. Left to myself, surrounded by louder, stronger, bigger personalities, my default was insecurity. This is not a statement about school systems. It just shows how impactful our environment and experiences can be!

I can still default to insecurity. I still battle it in my closest relationships. Do you relate? We can be *so confident* when we are around strangers or coworkers or distant friends, but with those closest to us, we hold back. Showing our inner thoughts and feelings leaves us exposed and unsure. I still have days where I feel like telling Josh something very personal, but am not sure how he will take it, so I keep it to myself. Something that could have drawn us closer is hidden away, all because of insecurity.

In Christ, we are completely secure. And I'm not just talking about salvation! We have His approval, His love, His presence, and His provision. These are like a spiritual security blanket when we feel vulnerable, but knowing this about Jesus only helps if we actively choose to trust Him.

Having lived with this battle for most of my life, I've developed a plan of action when I sense myself getting insecure and thus, withdrawing away from those closest to me:

- **Recognize** what I am feeling for what it is. If I start to feel anxious or nervous, if I start to pick apart what I am wearing or want to escape, I stop and ask, **why**? Whose approval do you want right now? What are you afraid of? What do you wish would happen here? Pinpoint the source of insecurity.
- **Stop** and pray about the source. If the source is a person, I stop and pray something like, "Lord, I am comparing myself to this person and it's making me very anxious. I feel like I'm not enough. But your word says that I am loved by You, that you approve me, and that I am no longer working for the approval of man. It doesn't matter what this person thinks about me. I am Yours, and I will live like it."
- **Command** my feelings to fall in line. After giving my situation to the Lord, I take a very important next step - something I do daily. I command my emotions to fall in line with truth: "I feel insecure right now. I feel anxious right now. But insecurity and anxiety are not who I am and they do not dictate my actions. I am confident, and I am at rest because I know who I am, and no one else's

opinion can change that.

- **Choose** to trust Christ. This is sometimes minute by minute. When I feel the feelings creeping back I take myself away or walk to a corner and repeat the truths I shared before. This works best if you have actually been in the Word diligently! If you haven't, you're going to find insecurity has a much greater hold on you. Seeking God regularly strengthens you for moments like these.

I follow this pattern in every situation, including when I feel insecure in my marriage. The difference in my marriage is that I communicate what I am doing to Josh. Letting him in on the process turns something that could have divided us into something which unites us. Admitting my insecurity makes me vulnerable, but it allows Josh to see the battle I'm facing and help me fight **for** us, not against us.

> *"He who dwells in the shelter of the Most High will abide in the shadow of the Almighty."*
> —Psalm 91:1

CHAPTER TWENTY TWO

SHOWING AFFECTION IN THE COMMUNITY OF FAITH

Most of this book has centered on our closest relationships - husbands, children, siblings, and parents - but affection influences relationships outside the inner circle, too. Your church family - the people who know and love you in the community of faith - will be affected by your view of intimacy as well.

Take a moment to ask yourself: "What is my reaction when people in my church love on me?" I don't mean the weekly greeting time (my least favorite event of any church service, ever, anywhere). I mean the people who are **in** your life, who know and love you, and who naturally want to physically and spiritually embrace you.

What is your response to them?

In the past, my response has been characteristically stiff. I didn't want to "do hugs wrong," and my trepidation came off as cold and uninviting. Inside I was screaming, "I'm just not good at this!" Even as my heart thrived on their friendship. Do you relate?

I've grown in this area, but only by doing three distinct things:

- **Staying in the word on this issue.** I know, I repeat myself a lot on this - but it's the one thing that will truly transform you. Your heart cannot change on its own. God has to change your view of yourself, the hurts of your past, and your view of love. That can only happen in if you are exposing yourself to Him through the Word and prayer!

- **Accepting love.** In my community of faith I tend to disbelieve people who seem to like me. "They do that for everyone," "They probably have tons of friends," "They don't really care about me that much." When I stopped letting my insecurity **lie** to me, and instead believed these people who truly cared about me, I was able to accept their love.

- **Stop thinking about self.** Oh, how hard and how necessary this is! When I'm getting nervous about who will approach me or hug me or how I should respond,

I'm really thinking about **me**. I'm not thinking about the joy it brings others to see me. Or the happiness at a mutual embrace. Or the fun of a lively conversation after a week with no face-to-face.

Have you ever considered that giving into fear of intimacy robs **others** of joy? That our struggle with affection isn't just about us, but about the people affected by our bondage? To me, that's a reason to be free. It's a reason to not just love my family well, but to love my church family well, too.

> *"Love one another with brotherly affection. Outdo one another in showing honor."*
> –Romans 12:10

CHAPTER TWENTY THREE

GRACE FOR US, GRACE FOR OTHERS

In Chuck Swindoll's book *The Grace Awakening,* he defines grace as "condescending favor." The root word for grace, in Hebrew, means "to bend or stoop." Grace is favor we don't deserve; it is God bending down to notice and love us when we have done nothing to deserve His attention! It is kindness, mercy, and love shown to those who are insolent, pushy, and demanding. The grace of God is beautiful, and the more we understand it, the more amazing it is.

But those who do not embrace grace cannot experience it. And those who do not experience it do not *give* it. Refusing to accept God's grace by holding onto our own "undeserving" is a twofold curse – it insults God, and it hurts **us**.

Grace manifests itself in countless ways. When we repent for our sin, God offers grace through Jesus. When we enjoy nature, God offers grace through creation. When we enjoy money to pay our bills, good health, and a loving community, that's God's grace upon our lives.

So what does grace have to do with affection? Everything! Our relationship to grace either gives us the courage to accept and give affection, or causes us to hold back in fear. A "grace awakening" in our hearts changes how we relate to fear. It enables us to give grace to ourselves as we grow comfortable with affection. It helps us give grace to those who don't understand our struggle with physical touch. When grace is ingrained in our minds, we're less likely to try to prove our worth and more likely to accept the worth God gives us.

Gracious living truly changes the affection game. It makes our transformation so much less urgent, and it helps us be patient with those who don't yet understand. But the key with a "grace awakening" lies in – once again – in our daily relationship with God. Since He is the author of grace, we can't know, live, or understand it without Him. If we want to grasp grace, we need to daily encounter the Grace-giver.

Have you done so today? If not, set the time and place right now.

> "...we are justified freely by His grace through the redemption that came through Christ Jesus."
> -Romans 3:24

CHAPTER TWENTY FOUR

WHEN YOU DON'T WANT GOD AS A FATHER

"I'm not sure I want to get married," The message read. "My parents' marriage was so awful, and my dad was so abusive to my mom, I don't know what a healthy marriage would even **look** like." Many of you probably resonate with these words. Close relationships scare you because the only ones you've seen have been fraught with conflict and abuse. If that's you, I'm so sorry. I grieve for the loss of stability and love that you must have experienced.

Because this book is for women, I want to touch on one particular relationship that can make affection difficult: The relationship between father and daughter. If you had a dad who was disengaged, neglectful, or worse, abusive, relating to God as a loving Father can feel foreign or even wrong.

My own dad is a wonderful man; I was truly blessed with a great father. In many ways he actually reminds me of Jesus! But due to other circumstances in my life, I struggled with my view of **god**. Not Jesus. Not the Holy Spirit. *God.* God to me was judgmental, distant, and not very nice. He was the guy from whom Jesus protected us. He was Someone I wanted no relationship with because He seemed to desire no relationship with me.

Clearly, my theology was a little screwy, because Jesus and God *are the same Person!* But when you're working through hurts from your past, it's hard to think logically and rationally. It's easy to let experience dictate "truth." It took years for me to really dismantle why I felt the way I did toward God. It took time to reframe my understanding of His character according to the truth - not according to my emotions.

Seeing God as the loving Father He is starts with what He says about Himself in the Word. Over and over He says He is faithful (Deut. 7:9: He never leaves), He is loving (1 John 4:16: He never abuses), He is kind (Psalm 23: He cares deeply), and He listens (1 Peter 3:12: He seeks relationship). Psalms is a great place to start if you are on this journey yourself! As I studied these passages I came to **know** and **believe** God's love for me - and this transformed my relationship with Him. I finally understood that Jesus was not "making up" for God, or a different Person than God, but that Jesus was the culmination of God's ardent love for the world (John 3:16). Wow.

Until we work through our view of God as Father, we will never be completely free from fear of affection and intimacy. This is a journey, and I do recommend biblical counseling, particularly if you walked through abuse! I can attest that digging into those tough places in my heart has resulted in a walk with God that is **more** than I ever hoped. I truly can call Him my father with love and affection in my voice. I do not see Him as an unloving judge but as a perfectly good and kind "daddy" who is holy and true. And this has freed me to fear intimacy less.

> *"As a father shows compassion to his children, so the Lord shows compassion to those who fear him."*
> –Psalm 103:13

CHAPTER TWENTY FIVE

INTIMACY WHEN YOUR SPOUSE ISN'T HELPING

Most of the women this book speaks to are in relationships with people (friends, boyfriends, or spouses) who are physical touch love languages. Perhaps this is what first revealed to you your fear of closeness. But for some of you, your spouse is just as much on the strugglebus of affection as you are, and it's a perfect storm.

I can't act as a marriage counselor in a 500-word devotional entry, but I **can** share truth from the Word and what the Lord has taught me through my marriage. Because of my emotional distance from Josh, he eventually pulled away from me. He didn't initiate affection or seek it out the way he did before because I didn't seem interested – and I wasn't. Eventually, my fear of rejection made **him** afraid of rejection, and there we were – two people passing in the night, never touching outside of our sexual encounters.

If this sounds familiar, you're not alone. It's hard to rework old habits and break old patterns. When you feel like the only one making a change, it's even harder. But if you want things to change, it starts with **you**. You can't control how your spouse behaves or responds. You can't control whether they feel convicted to bridge the gap between you. But if you're reading this book, clearly **you** think there is something that needs to change.

Intimacy takes two; that's true. But look at the picture God has given us regarding intimacy with Him. We didn't want Him. We didn't seek Him. But *He sought us,* and it was that pursuing love that drew us in. I wonder what would happen if we followed His model?

Now, I'm not promising you that with enough pursuit, your spouse will respond in like. We do not have that guarantee. But in most healthy, Spirit-led marriages, ones in which distance just "happened" over the course of time, healing is not just possible. It's **probable**! I frequently notice when I am walking with the Lord and letting Him overcome my fears, my marriage improves.

We grow closer. We hug more. We hold hands. And we **both** initiate it! But at the very beginning, I may have to be the one to do so - because I'm the only one under my control.

Ultimately, the key to getting your spouse on board with improved intimacy is to **pray**. Pray fervently for your spouse. Pray for them to feel your same passion for unity and love. Pray for God to lead them closer to Himself. You're inviting the most powerful Person - the Holy Spirit - to do a great work, one He has promised to finish in those who love Him (Phil 1:6). Nothing you say can convince your spouse to change, but by praying for them, the Lord changes your perspective and continues the work He is doing in your spouse.

> *"Do nothing from selfish ambition or vain conceit but in humility, value others above yourselves."*
> -Philippians 2:3

CHAPTER TWENTY SIX

PREACH TRUTH TO YOURSELF

"I'm such a bad friend. I get so awkward whenever anyone hugs me."

"My boyfriend is better off with someone who can actually love him the way he deserves."

"I keep letting my husband down. He needs affection and I don't even **think** of it."

"My kids are going to be ruined because I didn't cuddle them enough."

Do those lines sound familiar? They're the messages you're preaching to yourself on a bad day. They're statements about yourself - statements, that if not corrected, quickly become actions. Our thoughts are powerful. Even the secular world recognizes that we become what we believe, but only the Christian God gives the power to change that. We can accomplish much by willpower, but none of it will be stuff of eternal merit.

Because our thoughts are so powerful, we have to change how we think. But this is more than just "positive thinking." For every negative habit and thought we remove, we must replace it with a truth. As Christians, we have one basis for objective truth - what we preach to ourselves - and that is the Word.

This devotional is meant to make you think, but it's not the same as being in the Word of God itself. The Bible is a compilation of books, written over the course of hundreds of years, which reveal who God is and how He interacts with man. It is proved accurate through hundreds of fulfilled prophecies, historical facts, and the testimony of eyewitnesses. The Bible, then, is our basis for what is true. We can't preach truth to ourselves without it.

This is why I constantly remind you to seek the Lord in His Word! You cannot overcome a fear of intimacy if you are separating yourself from the one thing that would transform you. If you believe you don't have time for this, my friend, you're saying you don't have time for transformation! You don't have time for the love and faithfulness of God! You don't have time to preach truth to yourself - the kind of truth that would set you free.

If you've come this far through the devotional and haven't made time to seek the Lord in His Word and prayer, stop now and choose a time for each day in which you will do so. Need a place to start? The book of John. Take a chapter a day - or less - read, and take notes. Ask "Who is God?" And then think about how you can apply it. Then **pray**! Tell the Lord your gratitude, your thanks, your praise, your needs. Tell Him the lies your heart is telling you, and let Him replace them with truth.

> *"Sanctify them by the truth; Your word is truth."*
> –John 17:17

CHAPTER TWENTY SEVEN

THINK ABOUT SUCH THINGS

In his letter to the church of Philippi, the apostle Paul told the church what kinds of things with which they should fill their minds. Our fear of intimacy is largely a battle in our heads - a battle of truth against lies. As we talked about in the last chapter, it is **vital** that we inundate our minds with truth!

But what kinds of truth? Here's what Philippians 4:8 says:

"Finally, brothers and sisters, whatever is true, whatever is noble, whatever is right, whatever is pure, whatever is lovely, whatever is admirable—if anything is excellent or praiseworthy—think about such things."

What is true about you and your character? What is noble for you to do? What is the right thing in this situation? What is the pure thought about yourself and about others? Our understanding of what is admirable and excellent and praiseworthy comes from the foundation of God's Word.

When you consider yourself, your spouse, your relationships, or your struggle to show love, do you constantly dwell on the negative? Do you focus on your failure? Do you preach lies to yourself? Or do you think on what is good, true, and admirable - the hope of Jesus for your life?

Every day I make the choice to be affectionate the same way my God is affectionate toward me it's a battle in my mind before it's a battle in my heart. And what I put into my mind through movies and **tv** and books and even friends has the power to change my life. I must be so careful to protect my mind from false romance, comparison, and twisted perceptions of what I am supposed to be as a woman. I am protected best when I root my mind in God's Word - and so are you.

Living with a mind-check against the purity of God's Word will help us see ourselves in the right way, which in turn helps us overcome our fears, step up, and give love beyond what we thought ourselves capable of giving.

"Finally, brothers and sisters, whatever is true, whatever is noble, whatever is right, whatever is pure, whatever is lovely, whatever is admirable—if anything is excellent or praiseworthy—think about such things."

-Philippians 4:8

CHAPTER TWENTY EIGHT
AFFIRM YOUR PROGRESS

Two years ago Josh joined a hockey league. We had just moved to Michigan and in an effort to enjoy the winter, he decided to play. But the crazy part? He had never played hockey before! He hadn't skated in *eighteen years.* At first, he was like a tripod on the ice: Two stiff legs and a hockey stick!

I watched as older, more seasoned players spoke into his abilities. I watched how he listened and blossomed and how, a year later, he moved up a league. And even though he was still the most "beginner" player in that league, he made the draft. The encouragement of his more experienced teammates played a big role in his success.

There's something about affirmation that transforms us. It gives us the motivation to keep going, to do better, and to believe in our abilities, all because someone else believed in us first. I can't think of a part of life where this is **more** important than in our efforts to show affection.

It would be nice if our spouses and friends did the affirming, but we can't promise that to ourselves. At the beginning, you might actually get surprised comments like, "Oh wow, when was the last time you hugged me?" Or "Wow, that was nice! What got into you?" Having this kind of attention can be embarrassing, but don't let it stop you! Let it show you how much progress you are making. You're becoming a stronger version of yourself, and that's always a transition - not just for you, but for everyone around you.

Affirmation will sometimes feel undeserved. You might think, because you haven't been perfectly consistent in showing affection and overcoming fear, that you can't celebrate your progress. Lies! Celebrating your progress is **key** to momentum. If someone tells you they've noticed how you hug more, if your husband expresses joy when you kiss him, or you notice your kids cuddling up to you more than often - **celebrate that**! It doesn't have to be perfect to be beautiful.

Lastly, you play a big role in affirming your progress. Don't wait for others to tell you how great you're doing. If you've made an effort in the strength of the Spirit — even if others don't notice — rest in the fact that you took that step. This is one of the areas where I spend the most prayer! When I "act how I want to feel" and no one notices, I tell the Lord about it: "God, I purposely hugged Josh today. He didn't notice, but I want you to know I'm doing this for You, even if he doesn't see it. I know you see and approve of me!" It's like our little secret - a place I know I'm approved even when it takes my husband a while to see what I've been practicing.

Have you let the Lord affirm you? Have you accepted His lovingkindness over your efforts to love? Make this a point of prayer today!

> "Am I now trying to win the approval of human beings, or of God? Or am I trying to please people? If I were still trying to please people, I would not be a servant of Christ"
> -Galations 1:10

CHAPTER TWENTY NINE

CHANGE THE NARRATIVE

Changing how we think changes how we act, which changes the narrative being written about our lives. Sound good to you? It does to me!

As I look at where I am today in my marriage and friendships, I remember the person I was five years ago: Scared, angry, and full of walls. I was protecting myself behind a critical spirit and sarcasm. I was delighting in what was wrong with the world instead of seeking what was good. I am very different today, and hopefully, I'll be even more different five years from now. But all that change began when I opened myself up to God's transformation and realized my struggle with affection is more than "who I am."

You, my friend, are part of something bigger than yourself. Each day you let your heart be sanctified by the Spirit, you're changing your corner of the world.

Faith was always meant to be walked out in community. When we let God change us, we can't help but affect the people around us! It's a domino effect of love. Our **only** role in this is to trust and obey. That's it.

It sounds so simple, and it really is. It's not easy, but every command God has given us can really be distilled down to those two things. Love the Lord your God with all you are, which means trusting Him. Love your neighbor as yourself, which is obeying Him. "Love your God" is an inner relationship and "love your neighbor" is an outward act (Matt. 22:37). Together, these two things change the narrative of our lives.

I want to speak over myself the truth of God and change my mind to echo what God wants. I want to love others beyond what I feel able, and that can only happen when I'm trusting and obeying the One who made me. I want to be free from my own past, my wounds, my fears, and my failures; I want to live a life of bold faith and lifelong obedience.

If you want this too, my friend, you know how to

get there. It's drawing near to the God who loves you. It's surrendering your fears. It's reframing your mind according to truth. It's pouring out your heart in prayer. It's taking the step of faith that is obedience. It's embracing those near to you before you feel like it. It's risking the kiss, holding the hand, and letting God tear down your walls.

It's trust. It's obedience. It's the narrative of our lives.

"He has shown you O mortal what is good. And what does the Lord require of you? To act justly and to love mercy and to walk humbly with your God."
-Micah 6:8

CHAPTER THIRTY

YOU ARE A FEARLESS WOMAN OF GOD

You've made it thirty days on this affection journey, my friend! I am so proud of you. I hope this little book has opened your eyes to things you never saw in your heart. I hope this has inspired you to walk closer to the Lord than ever before!

There is so much more I could say to you, but I want to leave you with the message I need most as a sister who struggles like you. You, my friend, are a fearless woman of God. Fear has no hold over you. It cannot determine your future if your life is rooted in your love for God.

Jesus Christ came to set you free, and His love for you is unchangeable. He went to the Cross knowing everything He would experience and through His victory, we need not fear man. We need not fear the future. We need not fear pain. No matter what people do to us, how they respond to us, how hurt we may be by humanity, we can rest in the Man of Sorrows, who is acquainted with grief. He recognizes pain because He experienced it. He comforts us, emboldening us to face the risk of rejection with courage.

I don't want to live my days planning around rejection, always avoiding difficult things because I don't want to feel left out. I don't want to get to the end of my life wishing I had held more hands, hugged more friends, or kissed my husband more often. I want to overcome my fear and live courageously. Do you too, my friend?

My encouragement to you is to root yourself in the Word of God. This will lead you to know the Person of God. Trust and obey the Spirit of God. Then step out in and do the **will** of God, which is your freedom! What kind of freedom? It's the freedom to love others fully. Freedom to be a person no longer a slave to fear. Freedom to live as an overcomer.

Take a moment to consider the last thirty days. What is one change you see in yourself? Are you more sensitive to God's leading? More aware of your fears? More active in your affection? Those little steps are something to celebrate! God loves even the smallest, faithful step of sanctification. It takes courage to have faith, dear one. Congratulations on your boldness!

Don't let this be the end. Let it be a beginning. Let it be the start of you living as the new creation Jesus has crafted: One daily step at a time.

> *"Behold, I am doing a new thing! Now it springs forth – do you not perceive it?"*
> –Isaiah 43:10

TWENTY WAYS TO GROW IN AFFECTION TODAY

Need some practical ideas for every day affection? Here are a few starting steps!

1. Give your husband a surprise kiss and hold it for seven seconds.
2. Invite your child, sibling, or friend to sit close to you on the couch and talk.
3. Hold you husband's/boyfriend's hand in the car.
4. Hand deliver a note to your loved one,

let them read it in front of you, and hug them afterward (I know, it's a lot at once!).

5. Tell someone you love them, then tell them why.

6. Use breakfast and bed time as a reminder to hug your kids.

7. If you have little ones (or siblings, or kids of friends) invite them to sit close to you while you read (to them or yourself) or hug them and tell them why you love them.

8. Rub your spouse's back at the end of a long day.

9. Make a habit of hugging in greeting - don't hesitate or think about it, just do it!

10. Ask God to reveal a friend you can meet with regularly to talk through the parts of your story you've been holding back.

11. Take your significant other's arm when you walk.

12. If you like your space during movies, lay your legs across your husband's knees instead of cuddling. Be touching in some way while you're together!

13. Not physical, but text a sweet message to someone you care about telling them you love them.

14. Greet your spouse/family at the door when they get home.

15. Put your head on their shoulder while watching a movie or sunset.

16. Make time to talk about how you feel and how your friend or spouse feels. They might not be used to hearing your feelings if you usually withhold them, so let them know it's hard for you to share (if it is). Make time for both talking and listening.

17. Show appreciation for things your loved ones do – with both your words and actions.

18. Be receptive to affection. This is a big one! Even being open to their love is a step of affection on your part!

19. Flirt with your spouse. Wink, make a coy remark, joke with him!

20. Put away the phone and really focus on your loved one when they are talking, even if it's just about their day.In these thirty chapters you've explored your heart and emotions in ways that were quite new to you. You've challenged the way you think, the habits you take for granted, and things you previously chalked up to personality. What a journey to walk through in a month!

This is not the conclusion of your journey, though. It's the beginning. The questions you've asked in these short chapters will launch you to a greater understanding of God, yourself, and others. I hope you are more aware of your thoughts and emotions and more willing to step into the newness that is vulnerability. This kind of growth takes time and cultivation, but once rooted, it grows into something abundantly fruitful.

I hope the very best for your affection journey, my friend. May God bless you as you go and strengthen your spirit to love others the way He has loved you!

Made in the
USA
Middletown, DE